GRACEFULLY RAW

~a journey into rapid self-exploration, sin and challenge~

written and edited by
M. Grace

Copyright © 2015 by Myrya Grace
All rights reserved. This book or any portion thereof
may not be reproduced or used in any manner whatsoever
without the express written permission of the publisher
except for the use of brief quotations in a book review.

Printed in the United States of America

First Printing, 2015
ISBN 978-0-9861926-0-9
Kick Ass Community Publishing
3513 Smugglers Cove Rd
Greenbank, WA 98253
www.KACpub.com

INTRODUCTION:

I have complied this gathering, this grieving and celebration of pieces of myself.
I have went through emotions wondering if I am really ready for this to be published, but here it is.

Thoughts cross my mind, about the intimacy I am sharing. This work creates feelings of vulnerability in me, and I've been concerned that certain friendships or relationships or family ties might be severed or damaged because of judgment of my words. I've decided to throw out the fear of judgment. I'm not afraid of loss. I have already lost and gained many things in my life.

These pieces come from many different times, places, circumstances, desperation, depressions, joys, laughs, aloneness, longing, sweetness and beyond... and beyond.

Thank you to all who made it happen. To those that supported me throughout the years and encouraged me to never give up on myself. I express gratitude to my griefs and traumas, for they have helped to shape me just as much as my joys and blessings have.

I'd like to thank my brother for helping me accept challenge and finally come to the conclusion that challenge is what helps me to fulfill my true potential. Challenge is a reality, and I will emerge from the other side, stronger than ever before.

I'd also like to thank my husband and companion, Q. Without him, I'm unsure I would have even ever started writing this. His support has been given freely, although I haven't always appreciated or accepted it.

I'd like to thank past and present lovers. Some are shit, and some are THE shit. You know who you are. If you don't, then you're probably both, beeotch. Just saying.

This book is sectioned into the seven deadly sins and the seven virtues of my life. I hope you enjoy this baring of my soul. No pressure.
Love – M.

Table of Contents

The Altar + Home

Lust + Chastity

Gluttony + Temperance

Greed + Charity

Sloth + Diligence

Wrath + Patience

Envy + Kindness

Pride + Humility

Death + Birth

The Altar + Home

Mother nature is not an object,
but she is a home, frame of mind,
mentor, guide, coach, counselor, nurse, doctor and
friend.

STARS

I will always remember the silence of the high desert and the way it consumed me like paper in a fire.

I will always remember the large sky with its endless stars, painting overhead to the end of the horizon.

I will always remember the coyotes howling on those full moon nights, and the break of dawn melting the rocks with a shower of purples and pinks.

I will always remember those moments that have been burned into my mind through childhood.

Those were the simple days; and looking back reminds me of a beauty created, floating into infinity, long gated serenity.

Those were the days, I'll always remember.

-2006

IN THE HEART OF THE DESERT - AND SO I WAS BORN:

I was born in the high desert of the Southwestern United States, but I was conceived high in the Colorado Mountains, 13,000 feet elevation. My mother said it was a blessed day, for truly my father wanted only to give her one chance at a baby, and I took her womb over with such fierceness that she knew the very moment of my existence inside of her body. So obvious was my translation of purity, that she had morning sickness the very next day.

I don't mean to sound conceited, but as a child, I know I was meant to be here, for a purpose. I have a memory of myself watching my own birth before I was ever born. I used to think all humans were driven by this idea of "purpose", but over the years I have experienced that is not really the "normal" way of being.

Many people are content being numbed out, keeping up with the Joneses and typically avoiding meaning. My mother and father raised me outside of the box, never allowing me to blindlessly follow, never allowing me to transfix myself as the image of a sheep. I have always been a wolf.

Living in the high Mojave desert with her never-ending quiet, silence so pure that I could hear my heartbeat every day, and it kept me alive and real and unable to deny my humanity or existence. I was educated by my own intense and fearless drive for knowledge and meaning. I was unexposed to the world of computers, TV, standard classrooms, rude children or violence. I was free of the jaded feeling of self-hatred. "Heart", a half-breed coyote-dingo dog was my best friend and companion, my guide and my teacher.

The desert was so vast, that I could not imagine an end to the world, to the possibilities of what could and did exist. The bright and hot orb that is the sun, shone down and cast heat, starting a fire inside of my heart, mind and spirit. The cold darkness and the soft-glowing ivory moon held it's place in the sky and cast down dreams.

The moon rotates through the sky on an 18 year and 11 day cycle. I had a small window by my bed, where the moonlight used to shine in. Because of the anomaly of where I was and when, the Queen, Luna, filtered my dreams with psychic visions and ancestors. I remember frequently waking up in the dead of night and hearing the voices of the desert spirits, calling on me to do their bidding. To remember who I am and where I came from: a place I could no longer see.

Where spirituality comes as a journey that is to be discovered, mine has been blatant. I have never questioned the existence of another side. I have never questioned life before death or after birth.
I never asked for deep intuition or empathy, but I possess them with greatly mixed feelings. Holding in anger leads me on a path to depression, to hatred and irritation for all that is.

I was not a well child. I suffered from many ailments, sickness and weakness. My mother-wolf was a self-taught medicine woman, but the real problem was never anything but drinking distilled water and growing up in a place that was too hot for my body's chemistry. Years later, I know this now. Deserts are a place to awaken the spirit, purify and detox... but they are not a place to live permanently. We left the desert finally, when I was 13.

My heart often aches for that place of silence and solitude in the desert, where tortoises, lizards and coyotes painted my mind with survival and to learn to thrive.

It is a place that no longer exists.

My homestead burnt down long ago, the desert dried up even more than a desert, to a dust-bowl, the crops in the valley turned to dust and the snow melted from the mountains. I can go back to the physical place, but not the place I grew up, because of humanity's addiction to oil, water and poolside resorts, global warming has changed the fabric of the landscape. It is not the place that I remember or hold so close and so dear to my heart.
-2014

Today I Hold Onto A Mountain

The sun shines from between the trees, and as we
come around the corner she is upon us, the mountain.

The fog that engulfs the curves at her feet is reflecting brightly- revealing
her upward shape towering into the expanse of sky.

The clouds swim around her, the snow covered jewel, mystical in her
call of coming back into the raw silence of wilderness.

She is complete in herself and calls to me, the adventurer:
"Come into my arms, travel in me."

A shining chill flows through me as I gaze upon her beauty, how I wish
I could take her home, but only memories can be held.

-February 21st, 2005

Roar

The feeling is deep within me, the feeling of roaring a big goddess roar and dancing fire while drumming into my heart's desire.
Deep song of earth, smell of dirt, whisper of tree sprites and faeries spreading seeds.
Scent of spirits dancing on the wind, creating kin with all that this is.
Indigenous feelings and teachings rising up like mountains, solidifying like drying clay on hands that must be renewed.
Let's renew, let go of past pains and love all living things, for a change is coming like a heavy monsoon and we need to prepare for the plants taking back over after all these rotations of seasons, suns and moons.
Totem animals uniting in necessary cycles.
We don't know best, but nature does and soon we'll have no choice but to submit to the soil, water and solar magic singing their unheard song.
Sweet surrender to nature, I let go of fear and let the mud take me in her arms while she sings her sweet lullaby.
Roar Mother Nature and sing for all that you represent!
Reclaim yourself!
I welcome it as dear as rebirth.

August 24, 2011

I am so tired and ready for another big lesson... go home early and enjoy sleep in an empty, spacious, quiet bed.
October 18th, 2010

Memoirs of Dangling My Feet Off the Ledge

I remember over 10 years ago, when I was about to embark for my first time to France, a guy I barely knew then asked me if I was jumping off the ledge, I told him "No, I am just dangling my feet off".

Here I am now, a little over 10 years later about to move to France, not just visit for a few weeks, and right at this moment I am dangling my feet off the ledge about to jump. I'm jumping into an experience my whole being tells me is part of my destiny, and I have no idea what that means except to take it as a grand and glorious gift.

It is in this moment, that I am letting go of old things I thought made me, me.

Fabrics, textiles, trinkets I thought were the glue holding me together. I am saying goodbye. And even the leftovers of my life, that are going to fit in my 5X5 storage unit are looking back at me…
pages and pages of writings.
Sad poetry, happy memories, loss, gain and frustration of not knowing what it was I was supposed to be doing then.
As I look at each, smelling the scent of the paper, of ink of years past, I am reminded that I am more than the paper of scattered thoughts and forgotten dreams… of bucket lists and letters to the divine.

I am looking at all these things as if I am saying goodbye forever, even though I know it's not. But maybe it is goodbye… goodbye from the person who sits here now, who is undoubtedly going to come back changed, and maybe more changed than I can think possible.

I feel it is only natural that some deep piece of myself is mourning, and not just for the present, but for the young girl I was 10 years ago.
It is all a reminder of what changes, and how it is that each and every one of us find, adventure and create the people we want to be.

I am in an immense state of jumping off that ledge into trust… trusting myself, trusting the present, trusting the future, trusting my partner.

And and I am filled with a joyous and extreme feeling of gratitude and have a feeling that every hardship, every moment of my life has brought me to this moment!

When isn't that true though?

It is all beauty, blessings, adventure... a wondrous journey into myself, and an exploration of sharing life changing days, weeks and months with a human being I love so much.

I can only pray this isn't a dream... I feel a sense that everything has been worth it and will continue to be because the shaping and definition that is part of my being right now is unexplainable.

How fantastic to experience such loss and such gain at the same time! To be both terrified and excited to the point I feel my heart may pop!

-December 2010

Homesick on the Cold, Wet Grass

Paris… when someone says that word to any other adventurous young woman, perhaps the ideas would be the same as they were for me. Exotic, romantic, different, beautiful, intriguing, mystical.

There was some idea planted in my head over the years that one should seize such an opportunity with delight and excitement, never even stopping to think about what it could mean. For me, I knew it meant a learning experience and a discovery.

I have been here for a month and the blind ideas I had before my departure overseas have transmuted. So much is clearer now. I have learned so much already, and kept so little track.
I uprooted myself for the opportunity, and I'm happy I did, although I gave up everything I created back in Portland over the last 10 years.
I haven't given up myself. I didn't give up my friends, they flocked to me. They told me things I never imagined I'd hear, but things they wanted to say for years and then, thinking they would never see me again, spilled out their hearts to me with such ease I cannot help but experience extreme gratitude and compassion. Why did they act like I would be leaving for forever?

Today is a a bright, beautiful, chill, sunny, wintry day. I went to the little island by my apartment and took off my shoes, despite the cold, to attempt to ground again. How can a body know where it is really, if there is no contact with that world and place? When rubber, leather and concrete separate us from our place on this planet how are we to know where we really are? Or, for that matter, and a better question, who we really are?

With the extraction of my words onto this paper, I can feel the meditation inside of me, the quiet as I release all the noise, the ideas, the beauty and the intrigue I want to share with the world.
Passion seems to equal pain + compassion. There is no separation from one another, it is an illusion and has always been an illusion.
I invite you to walk, in the cold, wet grass… barefoot. Ground with me, where-ever you are, and remember.

-February 2nd, 2011 at 5:25am

Transitioning back to being an American, after becoming a European

It seems since I've come back to the states, that my opinion about Paris continuously changes. One moment I am reminiscing about the experience, and the next remembering all the things I didn't like about it.

I think the most important thing I've come to realize is that many people have a continued idea of "romanticism" when it comes to France. I've often heard things like "BUT you were in France, and that should be enough." and it's somewhat disturbing. As if just because it's Paris, it somehow makes it better. It's like saying just because a person is in New York it's better. It's not. It IS different, but what makes a place romantic is not the place itself, it's the experience of the place and the welcoming of others in that place. It's about community and communion, connection and compassion.

Paris by itself is much less than romantic for the most part. I mean, there is nothing romantic about the continuous attention a person must pay to make sure they don't step in dog poo while walking down Parisian streets. Nobody ever seems to pick up after their dogs, and so it is often like walking through a cow pasture, although I would much prefer to step in cow poo over dog poo. Don't even get me started about the metro... it is SO dirty, I often wondered if it had EVER been cleaned. Trash piles up and the air is dirty and smelly. The class divide is thick and poverty is prevalent.

Yes indeed, most stereotypes about the French are actually about Parisians. And yes, most of them are true. Many tend to be rude towards Americans... and yes, I understand that the extent of my French is: Hi, Bye, Good Evening, Thank-you, You're welcome, the ability to order food, as well as "I don't understand", I don't speak French" and "Do you speak English?" but I also tried to learn, and every time I would try, I would be cut off with English, and the school wanted to charge me double for French classes.

The general frustration I experienced around communication was nearly unbearable, and made my extent of exploration on most days be somewhere between a park visit and an eclair. The occasional seine walk or a visit to Notre Dame (the tourist district) was about all I could handle without feeling like a complete fool, even if the super-aggressive School for the Deaf girls would swarm me to try to convince me to donate 20 Euro . Even the Eiffel Tower area was unacceptable... as I'd usually be accosted by a dozen or so souvenir sellers. That was the point I learned to say "Don't touch me." I once went to the natural market only to have the cashier bitch at me about how little French I spoke, in English. Nice, real nice.

I've become de-socialized over my travels, or maybe just de-Americanized. I find myself at a loss for words when I'm around people, often forgetting the timing of when it's OK to speak. So little interaction with people over such a length of time forced me to work on personal issues and growth (which I am thankful for), but it also retarded me a bit in my conversational skills. It's not easy to meet people in Paris.

However, aside from all that, I miss my lonely corner of the park. I miss being able to walk by panhandlers and say I don't understand. I miss having no idea what people are saying so I can focus on reading or writing. I miss the food, the pastries, the outdoor market. And, strange as it is, I actually miss the filthy transportation system, because it made it easy to travel while it was raining. I miss seeing people walking home with nibbled baguettes. I miss laughing about the high class French walk (the way the girls swing their hair and their hips while walking in way too high high-heels.).

In so many ways, I feel my experience has displaced me. I no longer really understand where I'm "supposed" to be. What does that mean anyway? I feel I've gained an incredible amount of perspective and diversity and yet I have no idea what to do next. I've never had so much free time. I've never felt so free and so confined at the same time. I just keep looking for a job and finding nothing. I do want to work, and yet I fear the same abuse from an employer that I experienced last workload. My biggest question is whether or not I'll be able to stay in Portland. Financially, emotionally and other ways as well. Do I belong here and is there room for the new ideas I have, the new knowledge I'd like to share? Is there room for me in my partner's busy life? What will I do for income? Is there any room for me here?

-April 11th, 2011

Lust + Chastity

Never underestimate the power of a new relationship.
It can blind, numb, intensify, create, destroy and be the most
amazing weight-loss tool you've ever had!

Love requires kindness, compassion and caring like
a seed requires water, dirt and sunshine.
Without them it will never thrive.
Like a seed turning to weed, love turns to obsession

Finding the perfect mate is like
finding the perfect pair of dancing shoes, neither exist.
And, when all else fails, go barefoot.

AND SO I UNDERSTOOD MY PREFERENCE

I have never been a monogamous person. I tried for 8 years and failed miserably, tearing apart a heart of a dear friend, Wrist (name changed to protect the innocent), that was forced to take the place of "partner".

I remember being confused as a child by movies in which a character was forced to chose between one and another lover. It never made sense to me, and I never understood that there was a choice. When I was 14, I was in love with two different boys, and my mother said I had to make a choice, or else break it off with both of them, lest their hearts be broken. Bless my mother, for she did not understand me then, and my confusion of the situation led me into an eating disorder, one hidden by the fact that I am half Croatian and have a very sturdy Eastern European frame. Deciding not to eat lessened the pain that the world would not accept my inhibitions or preferences. The emptiness in my own belly, decreased the awareness of the other empty places. I felt so sure that I would never be able to love girls and boys and as many as I wanted without some kind of awful consequence. Eventually, I broke it off with both of them.

A few years later, things became more clear. I was in a long-term monogamous relationship by then, with the aforementioned Wrist. It was never pretty, how much my drive wanted to expand. By then, I knew I was queer, much to his dismay. He was neither aroused, nor amused by my sexual preferences. I was mostly in the closet, until I came out of the car. I was driving my brother and dad somewhere, looking straight ahead on the freeway, I just blurted it out "I'm bisexual- I like girls and guys". My Dad laughed heartily "Yes, I know. I wouldn't want to have sex with men either, men are a bit gross." My brother just sighed, "You'll get over it." I could hear my mother speaking from her urn, but I couldn't make out the words. It always took her awhile to accept things.

I kept cheating on Wrist, I couldn't stop myself. I always warned him. We rarely had sex, maybe once every one or two months. I was never monogamous. I frequently said I should live somewhere else, in my own apartment. There was too much emotional attachment and I could never do it. Wrist wanted to move back to Portland, where he grew up. I hated what I knew of Portland. Eventually, I gave in to moving, because I hated where we lived even more.

Portland ended up as the catalyst to my new life. My awareness of new and natural feeling options was expanded. Polyamory. I began to live my life, founded a bisexual woman's group and began exploring kink whenever I could. I never consciously hid anything from my relationship, but we were both in denial. His desire to move to this hedonistic place swept me away like a long-lost lover.

Eventually, after we built up the whole white-picket fence life, and had the dog, car, furniture, house payment, ice maker in the refrigerator thing, I started eating only whole foods and dropped 40lbs, then I left. It came without warning after I met a married man who was living the polyamorous life. It was just making out and touching, and it was better than anything I had felt in years. I didn't warn Wrist this time, I just rented an apartment so I couldn't change my mind, signed the lease, came home and told him. I was free.

I dated a lot, I needed to make up for the youth that I had lost. I finally had partners in my life that banished dependency and jealousy.

I had a lot of sex with only a few people, but they opened my body to new possibilities and ways of feeling.

I didn't know I could have multiple orgasms with partners.
I didn't know how good my body was capable of feeling, or how much pleasure could fill my being.
My whole body ached and the hatred of my body and old life shattered.

I was allowed pleasure. I was bound and tied, fucked, sucked and swallowed. My past reality crumbled and dissolved, a new one forming in the distance, and me in between, lost in a forest where Gods and Goddesses would seduce me into their nests. I was deliciously taunted and teased, my moans becoming music, my chant, my meditation, my prayer. What better prayer, then one of gratitude and delight? What better prayer than a unison of souls celebrating their flesh and desires?
-June 2014

Loneliness is the aching and desire for another,
the state of wishing for something to be different.

Aloneness is the acceptance of oneself, and current state of being. Deep within, it is the balance of self-support and inner nurturing. It is to be fully alive within oneself and fully present within oneself. Why would I want to change the acceptance?
Why would I want to muck up this feeling with anything else?

I am excited for my aloneness. I am excited about what it is and will make me capable of. It is an amazing feeling to be fully comfortable within myself and not have the desire to change anything for anyone except for myself.

Aloneness is self-love where there is no urgency for connection, no neediness, no desire to change the other to something else. Unconditional free flowing love that knows that there is a beginning, a middle and an end to everything, and it is OK to let go of the expectation and attachment that has been so prevalent in our society.
It is about relating, though love.

Not to be dependent on others and not to have others dependent on me is a wonderful thing right now. I can be fully present in every moment knowing that I do not have to change anything, or try to hold onto any moment. I can let the energy rush through me and leave a sweet essence behind that soothes my soul and lets it know that I am always at home, wherever I am.
Being in this space allows me to free myself to the experience of the moment.
It allows me to stop hiding anything, to let go of shame, and to just be present with whatever is in that moment,
knowing that nothing is permanent and nothing has to be compromised.
It is to live in a state of pure bliss.

A mentor, Neo, tried to explain it to me once, but I didn't know what he was talking about. I do now. I have released myself from co-dependency and have become co-committed with my higher self.
-November 17th, 2011

Bliss

Bliss.
Sweet unexplainable bliss.
My heart is pounding and I can feel the grounding you create.
Bliss.
Formulaic delicious bliss.
My smile is wide and my body takes a stride.
Bliss.
Daring brilliant adventurous bliss.
My breath quickens and I take a swift energetic burst of energy from you.
Bliss.
Variable understated fast meritorious bliss.
Everything fades in a present moment of total intoxication.
Bliss.
Exquisite attractive stunning wondrous stupefying bliss.
Don't ever stop.

-March 2010

Commitment

My relationship to and with humans continues to challenge me and bring about all kinds of interesting emotions. I cried tonight for the first time in several weeks, and thank goodness I had support when I did. It felt weird, but it also felt good.

I've felt numb to relationships and everything surrounding them the past few months, even avoiding them and everything to do with commitment. I've even been on a bit of a careless dating rampage.

I'm certain I've hurt some people along the way while trying to figure out what it is I have wanted, do want and want in the future.

My fear around commitment in partnerships comes from such a deep place of damage. I realize that in my adult life I have never actually had a healthy, serious (but still fun) long-term committed relationship. The key word here being "healthy". I have also found that there has always been an imbalance around feelings (either me or my partner feeling more invested in the other) and that it wasn't OK to express anything around those feelings without more pain. I haven't been willing to make myself or my heart vulnerable for about 9 months now, and more seriously 3 months. The pain I have experienced over romantic love was pretty unbearable... and I've continued to associate romantic love with heartbreak simply because of past experience. It has created fear, resentment and feelings of confinement, and, like a once wild caged animal, I simply have had a hard time visioning myself going into any room that looks as if there is a possibility to get trapped.

I'm visioning my pain and fear around romantic relationships falling away, and creating and facilitating healthy habits, communication and patterns in relationship instead.

Without all the stigma, I actually would really like to be available and go into relationship without the impending doom feeling of "oh shit, be prepared to get hurt". I want to work on that.

-January 23, 2012
(10 days after I met Q)

I Don't Want You To Be My Doctor

I am lying on the massage table, waiting, by request of my friends.

His hands are on my body as he coaches me
to breathe with his movements.

Slight adjustments here and there to release the complications of my
fitness, and of my shyness.

His hands are warm and skilled, touching the places that hurt and
forcing my muscles to release.

I am slightly embarrassed to be seen in this way, for I am vulnerable in
his grasp as our partners watch my breathy signs and moans.

His warmth penetrates my skin and I am left in anticipation.

He finds the sore places easily,
with affection and accuracy that teases my sensibility.

He massages my ears and pulls my hair tightly and I blush at my inability
to control my reaction.
Whimpers and sighs of delight escape my lips.

Intimacy is often difficult for me,
but I give in to the demand of his grip.

I am dominated in this moment, relaxed and willing,
receptive and wanting.

-April 2014

What Is:

Through all these years, I have yet to find a foolproof love.
Flavors of love, all tasty, undeniable.
So easily desiring to taste them all with all six senses.
Love rarely meeting middle, as twins, ideals, fantasies.
I reach out with my heart, wanting to give freely.
Please, please don't hurt me.
Consuming is the feeling I get when I look deep within.
Challenging, changing, aching, longing...
all these things create my fear of embracing.
And yet, I can't help myself.
As I fall into an ocean of emotion, I have to remember to swim.
When did this all begin?
I forgot to expose myself.
Variable me.
Warm touch there... then not.
Where?
An entourage of complexity.
Where is the light switch?
Present.

-2010

The Sex Club

Sex clubs are filled with alcohol and women scantily clad in their fantasies and self-worth issues.

I am confident. Maybe too confident.

I am a frequently in attendance. Working the club, picking up the dirty, lipstick smeared glasses.

My name-tag is like a lure to men, that I am approachable.
It is easy for me, because I get to both reject and accept them all.
They are freed from the fear of asking the
question of taking me to a bed.
I am glad in it.

I move through the dance-floor sensually and seductively.
I smile at everyone and lightly brush my body against them all,
so I can do my job more easily.

Sweaty business cards next to my breast.
I store them there until I can throw them away.
Sometimes I'll keep one just to ponder.

Fake smoke fills the club.
The smell of heat and sex and food is ever prescribed.
Pieces of confidence glow under the black-lights,
drinks that turn green.
Clinks of ice hitting glass.

Nervous couples leaving.

Confident sexy people closing doors behind which are well used hospital grade plastic beds.

I love this place, because I can, and it's finally allowed.

-May 2014

Ache

My husband makes my body ache when we are deep in our devotion.

I feel anticipation in the movement of his ravenous appetite for me.

He kisses my neck and I slip into our fantasy.
He is always willing to expand it.

The communication of our bodies is complex,
and often without words.

I feel his sweat trickle down my back as he grabs onto my hips and leads
with hard fast strokes.

I cry out in pleasure and pain.

Shivers of delight fill my body to the brim
until it spills over into him.

I ache and moan.
My orgasm ramps up and my inhibitions shatter.

My body ever yearning for more of him.

Desire fills both of our hearts and time falls away.

Hours later we emanate from our palace of sheets
and fall into a satisfied slumber.

-2014

Dating Is Stupid

He is sweet and kind and generous and chivalrous in a non-misogynistic way... and he loves me.
He doesn't say it, but I know he does.
This tall, thin, wavering, cold body and
sad gray-blue eyes tells me so.

But there is no mystery in it.
People who are not complex, or mysterious,
or hard to figure out do not interest me for long.

I feel his pink fluffy stupids of polyamory
sneak up behind me and attack me,
suffocating me until all I have left is the
ache of a newly charged sexual energy.
It tears out of me while I spasm to
depressing words and know how it ends...

With me bored and him broken-hearted.

I yawn after I orgasm.
"Fuck it", I think, but not like that.

I see my phone flash with his messages,
but I turn off the light, roll over and spoon my husband.

-August 2013

Complications in Sharing Her

The essence of my friend's girlfriend lingers in the guest room and I am sentimental.
Someone so young and also so old- in that wise way.
I remember the feel of her on my lips-
the salt of her tears after her moans.
Love, sex, sentiment.
And she loves me, she says, sandwiched between me and my husband.
Her hair is dark and wet from her shower and the coarseness reminds me how much gentleness she needs.
How will my friendship evolve when I have fucked her girlfriend and drank her like water and witnessed her process?
To maintain friendship and still feel her hard perky nipple in my mouth....
I hope.
I am filled with hope.
And love.
And more hope.

-October 2013

Love Lies

When did love become chocolates,
diamonds, bear skin rugs,
the sound of bling and so many other things
that only measure you commitments to a quietly
incognito system that feeds on feelings of lack,
and helps you to feel fat and afraid and undeserving?

What if love is not merely things,
but the unseen energy of a heart cracking open and
silently shouting peace and prosperity to all beings?

Love cannot possibly hide behind the valentines and
bouquets of roses-
nor, does love live there.

Love, much more likely lives in the eyes of a child looking at his
mother's breast for nourishment.

Or in the wag of a puppy's tail.

Love might live in the explosion of a moan filled with orgasm,
or the howl of a wolf at full moon...
or maybe even the snow gently falling on the forest floor.

Or a sunset.

But love certainly does not live behind the chocolates
and the valentines,
or the shimmer of a diamond in the jeweler's light.

-2013

Floating Moon

An orgasmic moan floats the moon,
and strikes against the longest curves.

Tingling desire makes the northern lights crash, then an echo of laughter
sways into the beyond.

A nova flares seductively in the shade of an eclipse.

A soft caress to the sun explodes, and the stars sing
to keep order in the darkness.

A deep breath dances against the heavens and comets
glitter across the sky.

Shocks of lightning cross the clouds and run away from night.

Morning wakes a distinctive dawn, which brings chasms of endless light
to reflect among the planets into the universe.

-2002

Gluttony + Temperance

Sugar is the root of all evil

FAT

I am fat.
I have always been fat.
At 15 years old, I had an eating disorder.
My ribs and collarbone were showing, no matter.
Still overweight on the chart they call BMI.
I was a fat child and a fat teen and a fat adult.
People judge my fat when I eat.
They don't say so but it's the little things that show it.
When acquaintances serve me food, they give me less.
I'm still fat.
I exercise myself into oblivion.
I scream and yell and ache, releasing all the poison that society dumped on me.
If I don't meet my goals, I punish myself.
My body hurts every day now.
It doesn't matter because I'm a masochist.
Sometimes a person gets tuned into wanting pain.
Some part of me enjoys it.
I have lost 100 pounds.
Still obese on the chart they call BMI.

-2014

Sugar

Sugar, always calling out to me and making me crazy.
The widely accepted and legal drug of choice.
Hiding itself in low calorie and low fat foods.
It is everywhere, tempting.
I have to detox frequently, like a drug addict.
My body sweats and I ache and crave sweetness in my mouth.
It takes two weeks for the symptoms of dependency to subside.
Three days later, I eat ice cream.
I have to do it all over again.

-2013

Delicious Satisfaction

Fat! You exist as nourishment!
I have been lied to for my entire life!
Cholesterol! You feed my brain and clear my mind!
Where have you been?
Why did you leave me alone for so long?
My body no longer craves sugar,
it is simply slimming down and strengthening.
The never-ending emptiness dissipates.
I look only for the humane and organic.
Meat, vegetables, nuts, eggs, dairy and fruit fill my kitchen and I no longer feel starved.
I am nourished at last.

-2014

An Ode to Apples

Apples to apples,
oh the sweet blush of the ripe, crisp fruit coming to fall.

Ruby, red, pink, soft yellow and green...
bursts of nature's honey sweet candy.

There is poetry in the fruit of Venus and
the so-called sin maker of mankind.

Only knowledge do I know of these:
Jazz, honey crisp, jonagold, pink lady, delight, cider.

I am filled with the taste of autumn, the final gift of fruit before winter
and the first gift before spring.

Apples, may I proclaim my love to thee?

By taste-buds on the delicious flesh of a natural creation.

-Halloween 2009

Cheers to Good Brew

Beer is disgustingly tasty, the glass all frosty, enjoy
the ale, don't be hasty.
It used to make my taste-buds
scream but as I grow older I like my beer much better,
much colder.
I'll order an IPA in the sun,
I'll order
a few more before I'm done.
The sound of a tinkling glass as it's put to the spout
and out comes a nice big stream of stout.
Ambers, Goldens, Darks, Reds...all
the colors of the beer goddess clear my head.
A sip, a smile, the tip of the mug...

We love our brew, through and through.
Without beer what would we do?
But my friends, I must warn you dear doe,
brew goes better in moderation so...
don't drink and drive or sputter and spout
or you're sure to end up
like old sauerkraut!
Enjoy your brew, your beer and
your time and raise your stein in celebration to the
divine!

-2009

Because all along it was only made up, drink from the cup

Sliced wine driven by intoxicated drivers.
Beautiful women encased in ecstasy, freed by the moonlight.
And me, wandering through the fields of the unknown today.
Yesterday, crazed, glazed by the sun.
Floating on through the clouds, a memory on the river,
naked, swimming.
Swimming through the thoughts of peculiar desires.
Glistening nipples in the starlight,
reflection of wants in the eyes of a stranger.
And here I am in the beaming of would-be painted memories.
Tear stained cheeks, reflecting waters, created desires.
One to choose.
Settling in the warmth of the candlelight.
It takes all my might to make things right.
Oh, the wine driven by the intoxicated.
It seems to make you hated, drinking from those glasses,
evil liquid of desire.
Addiction.
Swallow down the disarray, everything will be okay.

-March, 2005

Greed + Charity

MANIFESTATION
I dive deeply into the reflecting pool of my desires and my dreams.
The water embraces me, like a lost friend.
How can I rekindle this relationship with my deepest wealth?
Big, giant, humongous dreams that overtake my ability to sleep.
I am worth it, Universe.
But, do I believe it?

WANT

I reach out for all I desire... wanting, visualizing those things that have felt lost to me.
Imagining how I can obtain feelings and change facts.
I slip down the rabbit-hole as I drift to sleep.
Manifestations fill my heart and I wake up exhausted
for the adventures I have taken.
I swallow down my pride, like a pill,
so it can be digested and absorbed.
I am worth it.
I choke a little and know it doesn't mean less for anyone else.
I feel into my body, and breathe, and breathe in all the abundance that I create.
My heart explodes and fills my room.
I gaze out into the ethers, into silence, then crackling, then fire.

-2014

A Tragic (Happy) Christmas Fantasy

The conference room was very slowly filling with smoke. It was not noticeable immediately, as a slight fog was visible upon entry into the room... the smell of overdone pancakes, and non-stick omelet pans filled the air. The diners were eating merrily as could be for having to wake so early, and enjoying the processed pancakes filled with super-sweetened blueberries, and undercooked omelets. It appeared only to be a recipe for food poisoning, not the terror that was about to come through the office. I could hear the voices of the other workers, wondering if it was possible for the fire alarm to go off. Some wondering if they would be left in dismay, of pancake filled stomachs and the challenge of waddling down the fire escape stairs. Everyone so ridiculously sporting their wardrobes of holiday garnishments, holding their coffee cups. Half coffee, half eggnog sticking to their teeth, Christmas lights blinking throughout the office while management displayed praise via projector to those who were paid by hourly wage.

The most tragic fact in this story is not that so many Santa hats were sacrificed, but that the real cause of the fire was the alarm finally coming to the end of its patience.

The alarm did sound, very loudly, and the hourly employees ran to fetch jackets and towels to try to move some air and thus shut off the fire alarm. Alice, in all her glory, had a beautiful silk lined jacket, or at least it would have been silk, if she could afford it. It was not Alice's fault that she was trying to help, or that the propane lit omelet station was so poorly placed above the fire sensors. It took only moments for that cheaply made, imitation jacket to go up in flames. Alice was jumpy that morning after so much coffee and sugar, and the fear overtook her, causing her hand to reflex by tossing the jacket onto a grease laden trashcan full of paper plates, which was next to one of the tables decorated with crepe paper. The fire spread quickly as several of the other tables went up in flame. The employees were desperately attempting to put out the fire with water-filled paper cups. It was at that time, when someone picked up a cup of what appeared to be water, accidentally splashing it at the person on the other side, Melissa. Someone had been sneaking some kind of beverage that went up in

flame... perhaps some of the bottle of vodka from the gift exchange the week before. Melissa's silk Christmas scarf went up in flames, which in turn spread to her hair, at last tripping the sprinkler system. The sprinklers slowly put out the flames, and the employees sighed with relief, some looking down at their soggy pancakes, feeling thankful that it wasn't worse, as the water spread throughout the floor, slowly creeping towards the Christmas lights. Everyone was burnt, shocked and soaked and as the water crept for the tree and finally got to it, a shock rippled through the water. It wasn't a very well built building, there had been so many problems with the electricity, HVAC and elevators, so it should come to you as no surprise that the fuse did not blow, but merely electrocuted the entire staff.

As the stereo garbled "We Wish You a Merry Christmas", and lights flickered while the smell of char filled the room, I escaped down the fire escape, several untraceable bank bags of cash in my grip. I got into my car and drove off, just as the ambulances and fire trucks were arriving.

And I lived happily ever after.

December 27, 2009

Sloth + Diligence

My doubt kills more of my dreams
than failure ever can

Waking Up

My muscles hurt.
I've come to love it.
I love my body and my mind.
Please get stronger.
Weakness is leaving.
I am grateful.

-2014

CrossFit

When I started the transformation of becoming an athlete, I was resistant.
Out of shape and 29 years old. I hated everything having to do with fitness, except being outdoors. My brother encouraged me to try it, just once.
The first workout lasted a mere 6 minutes. My ass was kicked, I was sore for 3 days. But I felt something different, my mind was free of the worry and anxiety that had been there.

The pain allowed me to escape from the prison of worry, of what I couldn't control and allowed me to control myself. I hurt so bad after each session, those first 4 ½ months.

Sometime in the 5th month, my body stopped hurting so much, and all I could feel was strength. I still don't know if the pain transformed, I rose above it, or my body just finally got strong enough for the movements.
All I know is it felt good, each workout a meditation, a prayer, a celebration of my body and the things it was now, and would be more, capable of.

My body started to become firm, shedding off layers.

Each layer represented the pain and the difficulties I had experienced in my life. Those things no longer feel as painful. I figure that when I decided to push my body like this, it was the hardest thing I ever did. And fuck, I volunteered for this shit.

The first few months, I hated my coach, I hated myself, I hated what I was doing. And yet, I kept going back. It was not until I felt strong enough that I hurt myself.

I sprained my back seriously after double under jump-roping and continuous dead-lifting of 115lbs. 47 times I lifted that bar, and I hurt myself. I was out of the box for 2 ½ weeks. But when I got back, and started again, I found myself more strong than ever. An injury was not going to stop me.

It was that life changing conversation I had with my Dad over the phone exactly 4 weeks later.

He had called to support me, to encourage me to live my life fully and stay in shape. I was a bit angry with him, and I confidently told him there was no way I was giving up.

"I am stronger than ever. Nothing will stop me now. This is a lifestyle change, and it's permanent."

It was when I said those words that I realized I am in it for the long run.

I will never be the same.

I don't want to be.

The person I was before was weak.

I couldn't say what I felt with any confidence. I was living in fear. I was anxious about everything. I was angry.

Today, I am different. It wasn't that long ago, but it feels like a lifetime ago.

I am transformed, in mind, body and spirit.

My relationship is better for it, and I am taking the action in my career that I should have taken 5 years ago.

I believe in myself. I couldn't say that before, but I can say it now.

I believe in myself.
I love myself.

However, I am still working on that self-compassion thing.

-2014

Challenge

Yesterday I almost quit.
Thrusting heavy weight upwards from a squat to above my head.
A metaphor for all that I have experienced.
Why do I keep showing up?
I like challenge.
I cannot grow without it.
I get bored and cranky when there is none.
Jumping my rope in rhythm as my lungs cannot deliver.
Panic comes when I realize everyone else has already finished.
My peers shouting at me to breathe,
encouragement coming swiftly now.
Sweat drips down my face, my neck, my mind.
I yell at myself not to give up, that I am stronger than this.
I am not talking about the workout.
I want to cry and I do a little.
Almost done, I push through with everything I have.
Finishing, then collapse on the cushioned floor.
When I get up, I leave behind an outline of sweat and tears.
I did it.
It was never my body that couldn't.
Pain is just the feeling of weakness leaving the body.
Why do I have so much?

-2014

Getting Fit

I woke up angry because I ate too much sugar.
Hate fills me and I direct it at my trainer.
It isn't their fault.
Why must you push me so hard?
Right, because I asked you to.
I am angry and yell and cuss through my workout.
At the end, it's OK.
The anger dissipates and I love everything.

-2014

Completion

I couldn't complete it today.
I set my goal too hard and high.
It takes me 2 days to get over it.
Everyone says I did great.
The next workout someone else doesn't finish.
She did great.
I completed in a new personal record time.
Different challenges, different strengths.

-2014

Power Cleans

Hip-Hop plays over the speakers.
I am dripping sweat and tears.
I breathe in, hear the echo of my heart in my chest,
and put everything I have into picking up the bar,
firing my muscles.
In one fast and smooth movement,
I pull the bar up by entrusting my core,
arching my back and standing up,
trusting my hips out,
and bringing my elbows up loosely,
maneuvering the weight on the bar around my body,
rather than through it.
I bring my elbows pointing out, the weight under my chin,
resting against my shoulders.
"Good", my coach says. "Do it again."
I breathe in and start all over again..
In each moment, the movement of it, I find my power.
I feel invincible, although I know I am not.

-2014

Falling Away

Cellulite falls off my thighs, but my legs stay the same size.
My whole body tones,
but doesn't shrink, except a little off my waist.
I jiggle, but I am strong.
I am simply as amazon.

-2014

Try Again

The old me is breaking apart, into pieces.
I feel it in my bones, in my soul.
Weakness escapes me.
My muscles twitch and flex.
Internal boundaries roll up like an old dirty carpet
and are taken away.
What do you do when you are stripped down to your core, to a clean bare floor?
It's a different kind of fear, that dissipates and releases through tears and sweat.
When I fall on the floor, exhausted, I finally understand the purpose of challenge.
Doubt shatters.
Failure can't exist, if I get to try again.

-2014

Masochism

Every pushup, squat and stretch owns me.
My body is owned by my addiction to pushing myself hard.
I sweat. My breath is heavy and my head feels weightless.
Every moment of this torture that I endure makes me stronger.
I am healing the sickness and the worthlessness
that have been engrained.
So tired.
I push harder and harder each day.
My weight does not fall, as expected, but increases.
I am depressed and afraid.
I conquer it again.
Forcing myself to jump on the box again.
The pain in my body owns me.
Pain is just the feeling of my self-induced trauma leaving.
I won't miss it.
The pain is a solid reminder of what I am capable of.
I own the pain.

-2014

Wrath + Patience

When upset, breathe.
When you've had a challenging conversation, breathe.
Let things calm down.
Let things breathe.

Gratitude

I pray into the candle and smell it's sweetness.
The bees who worked so hard to make this wax, the worker who collected it and shaped it, and the friend who gave it to me as a gift.
I trace the symbol of healing, abundance and protection into the flame as I light it.
Increasing awareness, I pick up some of the sage from the place I was born.
Quiet, expanding desert, I could hear the blood running in my veins because of it's silence.
Fate was found in the light of the moon, while coyotes howled in the distance to thank me for being there. Life was simple then, and all I believed was true and my dreams shot off in the red-orange of the sunset.
All these things, I remember, as the sage smoke curls it's edges around me.
Please embrace me, dear sage, please help me to remember the simplicity and faith of my childhood.
I close my eyes and breathe in the aroma.
Gratitude. Faith. Gratitude.

-2014

Stuck in Portland Traffic

The Portland traffic sucks again.
I am stuck and the lanes are barely moving.
Yet, I am singing.
I am singing about ego.
Singing about perfectionism.
Singing about tragedy.
Somehow I am happy.
None of it matters.
Being stuck in traffic.
It's better than being stuck in life.
Stuck in ego.
Stuck in perfection.
Stuck in tragedy.
I am free.

-2014

The Raging

The raging storm of the weekend matched my internal process...
the storm within.

Sickness, deep aching lungs, I cannot breathe, cannot smell.
I am numbed and angry and wanting nobody, except the tears that run down my cheeks like old friends, each drop of salty emotional saline running out of my eyes, releasing the poison of all I have seen and internalized.
Like memories, they pool up on the hard cold floor, drip... drip... drip... drip.
My nose has been filled with the chemical ideas of waste and want... and it all comes out like poison, staring at me, reminding me that this is only temporary.
I am nothing and I am everything, and all that used to be flows away.
No, I am not my mother, I no longer have to swallow the damage of self-regret... or hold onto the fear of failure. I have already failed...
and like everything, it is only temporary.
Everyone I worship wants to change the world, and I know I probably won't. There is a knowledge, a backstreet, upstream, backstage, power behind the throne energy that knows that I, if I can embrace ego and express myself more fully and quit pretending that I am not wonderful, or worthy, or beautiful, or smart, that I can help other people in changing the world, which somehow feels bigger and harder and less glamorous and with less payoff then the alternatives.
But it's mine, and I own it, because I'm here and I can.
I know it.
I feel it.
I know it.
I feel it.

Drip... drip... drip.

-October 2013

Vengeance

Vengeance is inside me.
Constructing my own life, without a voice to clarify it.
Helpless voices calling out from the back of two young human's
self-made survival.
Tying an unbreakable, insane knot of thread.
It's inside both he and I, around our hearts, suffocating.
A whole mirror, that is yet broken and shattered.
Our tears pour with the rain.
I call out a name, but it drifts away with the wind.
The image of a sword lies within my lover's mind, trying to grasp
why must he fight so hard for breath.
A whole new universe inside my mind, a never-ending silence
makes space and wrecks destruction on internalized limits.
Reaching out for the real taste of life,
to be who I am and make life have a whole new significance.
I abandon the sorrow that we created together.
I glue the crumpled paper stars in my dreams,
and intend them to have meaning again.
Holding on so tight to my reflection,
as not to let myself drift away.
Maybe he and I were really trying to get revenge on ourselves,
and then make be.
Vengeance, a beauty inside me.

-2001

Envy + Kindness
(be kind to yourself, so you may be kind to others)

When a person is hurting, reach for their heart.
You never know what you might find there.

Do not discount the words: "I feel."
Those two cannot be debated or argued.

Progress

The moon is resurrecting old tradition, new completion.
A new paradigm, I know there is something new to express... but how do I express it? Is it an action, words, feeling?
Life, as ideas, like layers of floors in a skyscraper, awareness melting through all of the levels.
Define freedom.
Define nothing... for what really needs definition?
Experience all the way through from me to you.
Realize, till I can see across the universe into your eyes, with them.
What is this? Does it matter?
In this body, sweat, tears, laughter... divine feeling.
Connected in a whole new way, I feel all that was fall away.
There is a sweetness in my cells that radiate to my mouth and tongue and form a melting out of words that create a new free-moving web.
Conquering, truly, the skill of concurring?
My brain hurts, my soul aches, my body challenged to own this new vibration.
The time is now and waiting for us, it seems nobody has a watch.
I hear an alarm in the back of my mind, waking me up from a dream... or was that me being snapped into a dream?

-July 24, 2010

Healing

Healing is a place without a road-map.
So many destinations.
So many turns.
Does the journey ever really end?
A human condition of trial and error.
A human condition of beauty and bliss.
Healing as a way of life.
Life as a way of center.
I am healed by my own humanity and humility.
We're all perfectly scarred.
Remember to breathe.
How I love this journey with you.
Caring to be kind.
We are.

-March, 2010

Only use the words "I'm sorry" when you
really mean them.
Find ways of relating, for compassion is the perfect
companion to forgiveness.

Honesty is a state of mind that opens the door
to limitless conversation.

As I manifest my life through the energy of the Universe,
who am I to judge what blessings
and gifts it may bring?

Pride + Humility

Dear Universe,
Please ease my growing pains,
help me to be a smarter, more relaxed
and easygoing person.
Please help me to see the gifts in every situation and help
me to listen to my own advice.
Help me to channel my own truth and speak with the
clarity I am able to speak to others about things
unrelated to myself, for myself.

The more often I stop living in my head,
the more often I have clear intuition.

Alpha Female

I am an Alpha female.
Finally owning it is hard.
It makes me a bitch, I think.
Because I hold myself and others so high to their integrity.
My ethics often suffocate my desire.
Motivation.
Drive.
I take all my tasks with hardcore truth.
It's not that I'm a bitch, but I must have completion.
Alpha females seem dominant and hard.
Beta males cower at my feet in fear.
I stand up tall as I can. I am already taller than the average male.
Intimidating is what they call me.
But then, I meet the Alpha male and I am no more.
Only he can meet my truth.
Only he can stand up to my expectations.
Only he understands me enough to subdue me.
And we are.
I break a little, then we both howl.

-2014

Age Doesn't Matter

They say age doesn't matter but it does.
I am 30. Still people will tell me how young I am.
I hate it.
They say it to make themselves feel
more important and experienced.
I did it today.
A young woman asked if age matters in a relationship.
I told her it does.
We are ever growing and changing,
but the majority takes place in our 20s to mid-30s.
I think she was mad.
Her boyfriend, 20 years her senior,
yelled at me when I said men say it doesn't matter
because they like how mold-able you are.
It is true, and it's not true.
We are ever changing.
Some of us rage against the change and deny it.
Some of us are opposed to change.
Some just refuse to mature.
But age, it does matter.
It matters when it's combined with truth.
It matters when we admit that everything in our society says it does.
I have bought into the lie because I am older.
But they all still say I'm younger.
I wait until I am not angry any more when they call me "Ma'am"
I am not a Ma'am.
I am a woman, and I don't wish to be addressed this way.
It's supposed to be a term of respect,
but I hear it as a double edged sword toward my morality.
I wish I didn't know how old I was, or anyone else.
I wish the numbers that make up our importance would dissipate.

-2014

Bitch

A bitch is someone who doesn't give up.
Who won't take "No." for an answer.
The one who is motivated and ready.
The one who knows what needs to get done
and tells people how to do it.
When things get out of control, the bitch steps up to change it.
People don't like it, but they envy it.
I am a bitch often.
I like patterns and organization and completion.
It's my nature to stand in my power.
I enjoy the quietness after I scold people for whining.

-2014

Cryptic Metaphor Babble

The essence of self is not really self at all, but awareness and respect.

By respecting other humans we honor ourselves and create a new balance in the universe. We can differentiate ourselves by the gifts we offer and the skills we learn to use to help us grow.

We create toolboxes within ourselves and use the tools within to create the life and the awareness we experience.
Gaining new tools is not just about using the new tool by itself, but knowing that I can build something even more amazing when I use everything I have together.
The final masterpiece is a gift to the world, or sometimes another useful thing or tool...

And then there is the knowledge that I really don't know anything.

It's all memory in my hands and my emotions...

And then it just seems like I'm full of it.

So I cry, sigh, laugh and move on to the next project, hoping I can combine tools, skills and forces with others and create something entirely different.

There always seems to be a disagreement when combining tools... the faceplate here, this leg is too short, this leg is too long, this saw is too loud, I need an extension cord. Blah, blah, blah.

Once in awhile, when a pair, a few or several people get together with their toolboxes and all discuss and communicate a vision it seems to go smoother. There may be some edges that need to be sanded, but it comes out resembling something more recognizable and something less Frankenstein.

Then there can be a celebration, sometimes followed by a burning.
August 28th, 2011

Pain

It's all so ordinary and not so ordinary,
the pain behind closed doors that I try to block out,
that we try to block out.
The pain of the child, malnourished, missing his mother.
Later, his father, lover, friend, daughter, son, wife, self.
It's not real clear where the pain seeps to when it runs down the drain
full of sorrow and rage.
I only know it runs away from home sometimes.
I could see the pain in her eyes,
hear the regret in her voice as she laughed off the reality of his disposal
of her heart, that he never knew he had.
Fair enough, she disposed of him first.
Hearts ache, but push, expelling,
like a womb ready for the battle of birth.
We die alone, they say, but what if we don't?
What if we are jaded by the illusion of aloneness and the permission
it gives us to take a bath in the sorrow and rage?
We pay for it on our own, with our self-pity.
Take a tablet, a pill. Swallow it down. Drown out the sorrow.
I am not impressed, nor convinced.
What if depression is just compressed anger in the
mind that hasn't been released?

-2014

Never make rash decisions during a full moon.

SNAKES, HORSES and APPLES

There is a rather normal looking woman talking to someone in her own head-
having a conversation in the laundromat about the year of the horse...
"The horse is good luck for poor folks, like us.", she says, "out with the year of the snake... in with the horse, we trained them after all. Poor folks trained the horses to help us along the way."
Nobody is smiling but me.
I nod at her and agree...
Then she is quiet and gleefully watches the swish and spin of her laundry in the front loaded machine, like a child, until someone offers her a seat and breaks her tranquility.
She goes on about not wanting to be patronized to sit down, and about being independent and how she wants to do her own laundry, because she feels so much pride, all and of our best results start with quarters.
Then, I burn my fingers on the inside of a hot dryer and she scolds me for not having enough pride.
But maybe, I am the horse and she is the snake... or maybe she is the horse and we are all snakes, tempting one another to strike.
Or maybe we are all just apples, and the world is a snake tempting us to take bites out of one another, while the horse just stands by and watches.

-2014

A glimpse into the real Aloha

I have this deep intense feeling wailing up inside of me, a feeling of being fully grounded, of rawness, of what it means to be human.

I've been comparing my experience on the island of Hawai'i with my experience in France.

France was the concrete jungle... urban, starched, old, stiff, beautiful and in many ways, unkind.

Hawai'i is the real jungle, the heart of fire, remote, stretched, young, beautiful, terrifying and in so many ways, welcoming. Not for the faint of heart.

I spent the first week secluded on a farm far up the mountain, away from the experience of the island, sheltered in ways, away from the people.
The 2nd week has been the most raw experience of my life. I have met people who live in true poverty, but live with rich hearts and have such a passion for life, that it brings me to tears.

The sun slips down into the ocean each night and I look up at the stars and I hear these beautiful people...
Hawaiians and Haole alike, laughing deeply, sharing both their pain and their joy. The coqui (frogs) and the crickets and the sound of the rain and the jungle are my lullaby to sleep.

I have friends here who I would have never dreamed of meeting... who bare their souls because I listen... even though I am new. Every person I have met has shared their truth with me in some way, and I feel so honored to receive their story, to share in the richness of connection. I see the beauty in each person I meet... the reality, the goodness.

A new friend, took my hand last night and said "Why wouldn't you grab my hand? We're fucking human, why are we afraid of touch?."

There is such a rawness here. The poison sweats out of my body, seeps out of my heart, and I am torn open... not because of any reason but because the island says I must. I'm sweating out old ideals, old judgments. My body is strong, as I eat the mango from a struggling organic farm, I am nourished by their work. The remoteness of Puna, the jungle here, is like I have been transported to another time, a time very sacred.

It hasn't been easy. I have been challenged to face my fears and explore myself. I have had to face my shadow many times... this place, the rawness, has brought me to tears many times. And it is everything I have needed in each moment.

I looked over the volcano, answered to Pele, and had to face my own fire. Hawai'i brings out the fire in people, the passion.

I think about the people who visit here, for vacation, who stay in fancy hotels and never really see Hawai'i. They do not experience the true "Aloha", in my opinion, which is not fancy, but wild, untamed and dirty. "Aloha" is not something that can be explained in words, it is an experience of human to human. The call of the wild in the jungle, the bleeding heart worn on the sleeve of a culture.

I am torn apart, and I am being put back together.

If the island wants me here, she will keep me... and I wouldn't change my experience for anything.
I need to be here, to remember who I am and what I am doing on this planet.
I love this place and embrace being here fully and I want to leave this place with fierceness as well... and I will be here, until I am not here.

Gratitude.
Aloha.
Breathing.
Mahalo.
Gratitude.
Aloha.

-September 2012

Questions to the Self

May I hold the ocean in my heart?
May I burst from the weight?
And the moon by my side, as my smile?
Will the whole world end as I know it to be?
Will I still remember the girl I used to be?
And to love, will she swallow all of my sorrows?
Or leave my heart hollow?
Many years have passed, and still I wonder:
"What does it all mean?
Am I really here or is this all a dream?

-September 2010

Death + Birth

And so the Universe takes another deep breath, turns... and laughs at me.

The Winds Are Changing

Earth winds scent once dancing through roses.
Pastel flakes of summer laughter.
Rustic fields of autumn, touch the things that time has changed.
Ages walked through, like a dream.
Wondering where all the years have gone,
and why they tend to fade away.
Catching a realization that every moment has meant something.
All things are to be treasured and secured within the walls of the heart
felt beings that we have become.
Delicious essence of life is born.

-2003

My Mother Dies

When my mother was trying to die, my grandmother did not let her...

Grandmother's eyes and heart are filled with the regret of never really understanding her daughter's potential, nor understanding who she was.

My grandmother cries, not for my mother, but for herself and her sorrow, of never really knowing my mother.

She wants my mother to come out of her coma and say "I love you." one more time. A selfish and relentless wish.

My brother can not even cry, although only 12 years old, he will later grow up to be a criminal, then transform into a successful businessman and communicator.

And why is my great-aunt here, in this room?
To protect my grandmother from her regret, or to protect her from my father?

My father has been married to my mother since 1980- 25 years,

My Grandmother and my Father have hated each other for at least that long.

My Father looks at my Mother.
He loves her and he hates her.
Loves her for the spectacular woman she is
and hates her for getting sick,
aging rapidly,
and and her deep, dark depression for the state of the world.
She wanted to die.
And he will be left alone to pick up the pieces.

I feel I am the only one who knows my mother and
how deep she went.

I know the depth and the wanting of her departure and her journey and her passion,
and the love she always gave to everyone without question or regret or explanation- regardless of her grudges or the bad blood running through their veins.

Her body glows and although machines keep her breathing, I know that she is gone from this world, so tell them to unplug her...

She only finally dies, and takes her journey out past the stars, when we all leave and quit holding onto who she was
and just let her be who she is meant to be.

The greatest pain I can imagine silently and subtlety trickles through me for 10 years,
never unleashing it's full wrath,
because it knows that I will not survive it.
This is the way the Universe was kind.

Eventually,
I grow up and realize that the pain kept me going and freed me from self-limitation – because I understand how short life is...

I make up for it my deciding to embody presence.

My mother's death is also the greatest gift – like being born from her womb,
I am also conceived again in her death, and in-vitro for a decade to discover the greater gift of who I am.

-August 2013

Opening waves

I can hear your light whispering to me
through the cracks in the door to my soul.
Living, yet fighting the humility within.
Mistaken and regretted words I spoke to you
through the keyhole,
I thought for sure it would open,
but it needed something more.
I'm unsure of how I missed the point that
was being made, I guess I never thought it
would be so important to you that I were not afraid.
You are gone, and yet you remain legendary.
Death erases all imperfection, and I am pleased.
Disappearing into the water of creation, and
surfing upon life's wave,
silky shadows at sunset somehow turn to brightness and my
heart is filled with admiration, letting go
of fear, I let my gratitude glisten
on the crest, and hope that it will benefit
the world somehow.
Life has never been this important until now.

-2003

The more I process,
the more I see that I really, really don't need to.

March 26th, 2014

My nephew was born today. I have not yet met him,
but love flows out of me like water.

I don't need to meet him,
I already know that I love him beyond measure.

My small family is growing ever so slightly.

My womb is empty.

More and more I feel the pull of biology and
hormones beg me to carry life.

Instead I carry mixed emotions.

The chatter of parents and their ever challenging belief of their whole
world coming crashing down.

Everything changes they say, your child will be everything.
While I can see how that could be true.

I doubt.

Tiny, beautiful, young lives destroying dreams.

Does where a parent ends and a child begins become skewed?

Will I ever be ready? I don't know.

Tragedy cannot possibly come prepared
and prepped in a small blanket.

Need exists in the firm grip of a tiny hand grasping for care.

Biology

I finally meet him, my day-spring, my new, my nephew.

Love flows through me like a river.

My heart fills like a balloon, bursts, becomes whole and bursts again.

He shares my blood.

He smells right.

I howl. It is the full moon.

I am auntie-wolf and mother-wolf and woman.
He is tiny, and I must protect him.
His cries do not panic me.
He is adjusting to becoming a wolf-baby, too.
He howls.
He smiles.

I am proud. I feel animal and underestimated in my instinct.
I finally understand my purpose.
Family.

Always must I have my pack.
Biology demands it.

-April 2014

TODAY

Deep breaths, deep thoughts, today.
I learn something new every single day, sometimes not realizing it.
The death, the life co-existing within one breath,
the eternal breath of the Universe.

My heart pours out like rain, all over you, and I wonder what it feels like.
Beauty is an essence from the heart;
all that is created is beautiful in it's own way.

I hear the beauty and the life breathing into me, filling me to the brim
with the feeling of being alive.

The death that we fear will come no matter what, eventually.
I feel the eternal bliss coming from the soul, and know,
that life doesn't end here.
When we die, it doesn't end.
We'll all be going on forever, hanging on to our humility, our beliefs,
and our experiences here.

The drama we create in our lives, we life for, yet we hate it.
If there were no more drama, would we really enjoy life?

Experiencing, breathing, loving and knowing.

We are not alone, and we never have been.

The illusion of aloneness comes from within ourselves, not wanting to
except our humanity.

Humanity and humility co-existing, being the gift that keeps us going.
We are all here for a reason, have you ever stopped to listen?

Maybe it all starts right here, listening to each other.

-April, 16th, 2004

To struggle against the Divine's plan is
to drown in the rip-tide.

www.ingramcontent.com/pod-product-compliance
Lightning Source LLC
Chambersburg PA
CBHW032132090426
42743CB00007B/574